HANDS-ON
Science

Sound and Light

Jack Challoner

Illustrations by David Le Jars

KING*f*ISHER

KINGFISHER
Kingfisher Publications Plc
New Penderel House,
283–288 High Holborn,
London WC1V 7HZ
www.kingfisherpub.com

Produced for Kingfisher by PAGEOne
Cairn House, Elgiva Lane, Chesham
Buckinghamshire HP5 2JD

For PAGEOne
Art Director Bob Gordon
Editorial Director Helen Parker
Project Editors Sophie Williams, Miriam Richardson
Designers Monica Bratt, Tim Stansfield

Illustrator David Le Jars

For Kingfisher
Managing Editor Clive Wilson
Production Controller Jacquie Horner
DTP Co-ordinator Nicky Studdart

First published by Kingfisher Publications Plc 2001
10 9 8 7 6 5 4 3 2 1
1TR/1200/TWP/GRST/150SMA

Copyright © 2001 Kingfisher Publications Plc

A CIP catalogue record for this book is available from
the British Library

ISBN 0 7534 0271 8

Printed in Singapore

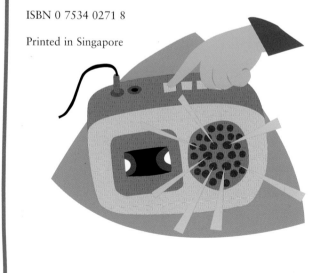

CONTENTS

Getting started

Sound and light allow people to enjoy and understand the world around them. But have you ever wondered what sound and light actually are? In this book you can find out. It is packed with activities you can try at home or at school, which will help you to understand sound and light and to realise how important they are to our lives.

See hear

The buzzing of a bumble bee, the blast of a trumpet, the roar of a jet engine, the crack of a whip – all of these are sounds. But just what is sound – how does it reach people's ears, and how do people hear?

A flash of lightning, the glare of the Sun, the glint of a diamond, the green glow of a traffic light – all of these are light. But what is light – how does it reach people's eyes, and how do people see?

What you need

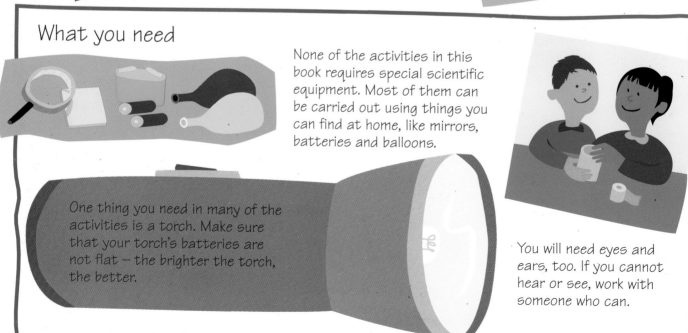

None of the activities in this book requires special scientific equipment. Most of them can be carried out using things you can find at home, like mirrors, batteries and balloons.

One thing you need in many of the activities is a torch. Make sure that your torch's batteries are not flat – the brighter the torch, the better.

You will need eyes and ears, too. If you cannot hear or see, work with someone who can.

Clock symbol

The clock symbol at the start of each experiment shows you approximately how many minutes the activity should take. All the experiments take between 5 and 30 minutes. If you are using glue allow extra time for drying.

Warning

Whenever you are experimenting, it is important to be safe.

Bright lights can be harmful to eyes. Never look directly at the Sun, especially through any telescope or binoculars – you risk being blinded for life.

Be careful when using an electric lamp of any kind. The bulb in this can get very hot and cause a burn or set something touching it alight.

Sound can be harmful, too. Try to avoid very loud sounds, especially for long periods of time – for example, try not to listen to music too loudly through earphones or headphones.

Having problems?

Some of the activities in this book can be a bit fiddly, and require patience and sometimes an extra pair of hands.

If something doesn't seem to be working, read through each step of the activity again and have another go. If there is something you don't quite understand, read the explanation again, or ask an adult to help you.

Do try all the activities – the more you explore what light and sound can do, the better you will understand them. And don't be scared to try your own versions of the activities as long as they are safe (ask an adult for advice). After all, trying something new is what scientists are best at! You may find out something new.

Stuck for words?

If you see a word you don't recognise or you want to find out more, take a look in the Glossary on pages 38 and 39.

Sources of sound

Take a moment to stop and listen to the sounds around you. Close your eyes if it makes it easier. Things that produce sound are called sound sources. Most sources of sound are objects moving quickly backwards and forwards, or 'vibrating'. The vibrations that produce sound are far too fast to see, but you can often feel them.

Shock wave!

Some sounds are produced by shock waves, not vibrations. A shock wave is caused by something moving very fast, like a bullet or a supersonic aeroplane. You can make a loud shock wave, using a home-made paper banger.

YOU WILL NEED
◆ ONE PIECE OF A3 PAPER
10

1 Look at the sequence of pictures that show you how to make the banger. You should begin by folding the paper lengthways. The dotted line shows you where to fold the paper.

A

B

C

D

E

F

2 Once you have made your banger, grasp it as shown between a finger and thumb. Hold the banger above your head and bring it down swiftly, as if you are hammering in a nail. As you stop, the paper fold flies out, causing a loud bang.

What's going on?
As the folded centre of the banger flies out at speed, it pushes air in front of it, creating a shock wave. The shock wave is heard as a loud bang.

Make a bull-roarer

Thread one end of the string through the hole in the ruler, and tie it securely. Use at least two firm knots. Go outside, away from other people, and hold the string, near the free end. Now, whirl the ruler around your head. You should hear a strange sound.

YOU WILL NEED   5
◆ A PLASTIC OR WOODEN RULER WITH A HOLE AT ONE END
◆ A PIECE OF STRING ABOUT 1M LONG

What happens to the sound as you whirl the ruler faster?

What's going on?

The ruler spins rapidly as you whirl it around. As it does so, it makes the air vibrate, producing the strange sound that you hear. The faster the ruler whirls, the more high-pitched the sound becomes.

Feel the vibrations

Gently touch both sides of your throat as you sing or shout. What do you feel? Your voice can also make a plastic bottle vibrate. Sing into an empty bottle, and feel the vibrations in the side of the bottle.

YOU WILL NEED   5
◆ YOUR THROAT!
◆ AN EMPTY PLASTIC BOTTLE

A LOUD BANG
Explosives are often used to help demolish old or unsafe buildings. The gases produced by an explosion expand rapidly, causing a shock wave. The bigger an explosion, the greater the shock wave, and the louder the sound.

Sources of light

Things that produce light, such as the Sun or a torch, are called light sources. The Sun and the torch bulb produce light because they are hot. This is called incandescence. Some light sources, such as fireflies and television screens, are not hot. They give out light by luminescence.

White hot!

Hot objects give out red light. If they get hotter still, they give out yellow. Really hot things glow white.

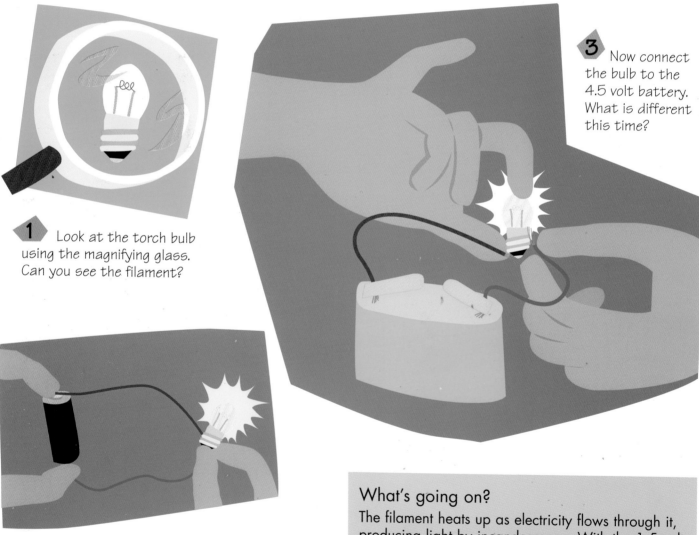

1 Look at the torch bulb using the magnifying glass. Can you see the filament?

3 Now connect the bulb to the 4.5 volt battery. What is different this time?

2 Connect the bulb to the 1.5 volt battery, using wires as shown.

What's going on?

The filament heats up as electricity flows through it, producing light by incandescence. With the 1.5 volt battery, the filament gives out yellow light. With the 4.5 volt battery, the filament is much hotter, and gives out bright white light.

Sweet light

YOU WILL NEED
- SUGAR CUBES
- A ROLLING PIN
- A CLEAR PLASTIC BAG

5

Place a few sugar cubes in the plastic bag. Find a very dark room. Stay there for at least five minutes, to make your eyes more sensitive. Now, crush the sugar cubes using the rolling pin.

What's going on?
There are many types of luminescence. One of them is triboluminescence, in which some materials give out light when they break. Sugar cubes are triboluminescent. When the sugar is crushed, the atoms break apart and give out blue light.

Can you see tiny flashes of blue light?

After glow
Make the room dark, and turn the television off. Hold the torch against the television screen. Turn on the torch for about a minute, then turn it off.

YOU WILL NEED
- A TORCH
- A TELEVISION

5

When you move the torch away from the screen what do you see?

What's going on?
A television screen is a light source. The inside of the screen is coated with dyes that can glow by luminescence. The energy of the torch light is stored in the dyes in the screen. They give out the energy gradually, producing a faint glow over a few minutes.

LIGHTS IN THE SKY
Fireworks make an impressive light display in the sky. The red, yellow and white flashes are produced by incandescence, while the bright colours are produced by luminescence.

Sound travels

The vibrations that cause sound travel in all directions as waves. If you shouted to someone standing 340 metres away from you, the sound of your voice would take about one second to reach the other person. Most of the sound we hear travels through the air, but sound can also travel through solids and liquids.

Air waves

YOU WILL NEED ▶ 10
◆ A JUG
◆ WATER
◆ A SHALLOW TRAY
◆ TWO PENCILS

Sound waves spread out in all directions, just like water waves. This is why a sound becomes quieter the farther you are from it. A megaphone prevents sound from becoming too spread out.

3 Place the pencils into the water, as shown. Make waves again, where the pencils are close together. What happens to the waves now?

1 Put some water into the tray. Wait for it to settle.

2 Touch your finger on the water's surface. Vibrate your finger up and down to produce water waves that travel in every direction, just like sound waves through the air.

What's going on?
The more spread out a sound wave is, the quieter the sound. The pencils in the water do not allow the water waves to spread out so much. In the same way, the sides of a megaphone do not allow the sound waves to become so spread out either.

String sounds

Tie about 40cm of thread to the spoon, near the middle. Wrap the free end of the thread around a finger, and swing the spoon so that it hits against the table. Now, do the same again, but this time put the finger with the thread wrapped around it into your ear.

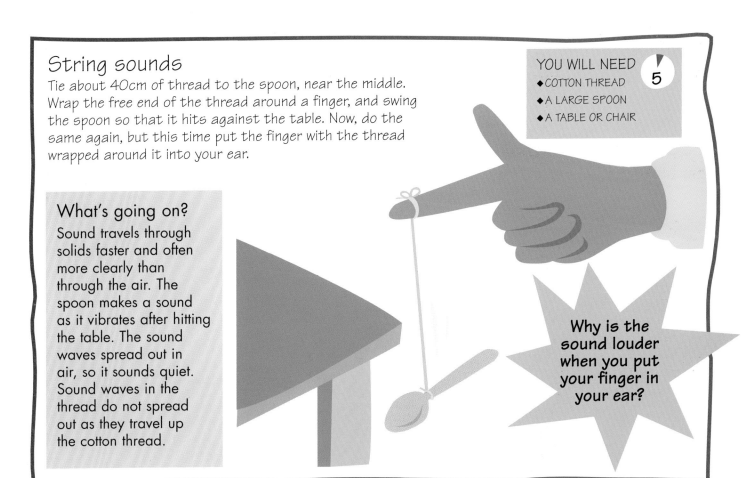

What's going on?

Sound travels through solids faster and often more clearly than through the air. The spoon makes a sound as it vibrates after hitting the table. The sound waves spread out in air, so it sounds quiet. Sound waves in the thread do not spread out as they travel up the cotton thread.

Why is the sound louder when you put your finger in your ear?

FLASHBACK

A sound idea

Probably the first person to realise that sound travels as waves was the Roman architect Vitruvius. Nearly 2,000 years ago, he wrote that sound moves like the 'waves which appear when a stone is thrown into smooth water'.

SHOUT AS LOUDLY AS YOU LIKE...
In outer space, there is no air. So, however loudly you shout, you will not be heard. Space is absolutely silent.

Light travels

When you turn on a torch, the bulb seems to light up immediately. Actually, it takes a short time for the torch light to travel to your eyes – less than a hundred millionth of a second! Even though it travels at such an incredible speed, light from the Sun takes eight minutes to reach us on Earth. Light does not travel through all materials. Where an object stops the passage of light, a shadow may form.

Seeing the light

You can only see light when it shines into your eyes! To do all these steps together, try this experiment when it is dark outside.

YOU WILL NEED
- A TORCH
- SOME NEWSPAPER
- TALCUM POWDER
- A FRIEND

5

Where is the beam of light going?

1 Put some newspaper down in a room to protect the floor, and make the room dark.

2 Ask a friend to shine the torch from one side of the room to the other, so that the torch beam passes in front of your eyes. You cannot see the beam.

3 Sprinkle the talcum powder in the path of the light beam. Suddenly, you can see where the light is going. What happens if your friend blocks part of the beam with a finger?

What's going on?
When light from the torch hits the tiny particles of talcum powder, it bounces off in all directions. Some of the light makes it into your eyes, so you can see the path of the beam. When the air is clear, and there is nothing to bounce the light into your eyes, the beam of light goes past you without you seeing it.

Passing through

Ask a friend to shine a torch in your direction, but not directly into your eyes. What happens if he or she holds different materials in front of the torch? Try clear plastic, tracing paper, wood, metal, and a hand.

Does light pass through some materials better than others?

What's going on?

Materials through which you can see clearly, through which light passes, are called transparent. Materials like tracing paper, which let light through, but that you cannot see through clearly, are called translucent. Opaque objects let no light through at all.

The Speed of Light

FLASHBACK

The first person to attempt to measure the speed of light was the Italian scientist Galileo Galilei. Nearly 400 years ago, one dark night, Galileo and his assistant stood far apart and flashed lanterns at each other. They tried to work out how long light from the lanterns took to pass between them. The only thing Galileo could say about light after the experiment was that it travels very fast!

4 Take the torch outside when it is dark. Shine it straight up into the air. Only if it is misty or foggy will you will be able to see the torch beam.

THE SUN THROUGH THE TREES
You can see the path of light from the Sun through the trees because of the mist. The light is bouncing off tiny droplets of water hanging in the air. The light travels in straight lines.

Different tones of sound

The sound of your voice is produced by small flaps of skin, called vocal cords, inside your throat. When you sing or speak in a high voice, as when female opera singers sing, your vocal cords vibrate very quickly. When you make a low-pitched sound, like male opera singers do, your vocal cords vibrate more slowly. All sounds may be high- or low-pitched, depending on how rapid the vibrations are that cause them.

Low and high

Low-pitched sounds are produced by slow vibrations and high-pitched sounds by more rapid vibrations. Listen carefully for the different high- and low-pitched sounds caused by the following sources of sound. Ask permission to use the hi-fi!

YOU WILL NEED
◆ A PLASTIC DRINKS BOTTLE
◆ A JUG OF WATER

5

What's going on?
The column of air inside the bottle vibrates when you blow across the top of the bottle. The shorter the air column, the faster the air vibrates, so the higher the note.

1 Fill the plastic bottle with some of the water from the jug.

2 Blow across the top of the bottle to make a note.

3 Put more water from the jug into the bottle. Blow across the top of the bottle again. How has the note changed?

14

High-pitched hiss

Make sure that there is no cassette in the tape recorder. Press 'PLAY', turn the volume up quite high, and stand two or three metres away from the loudspeakers. What do you hear? Now, cup your hands behind your ears while you listen to the hissing sound made by the tape recorder.

Can you hear a hiss?

What's going on?

When you play a tape recorder, you can sometimes hear a hissing noise. This is a very high-pitched sound, caused by rapid vibrations in the loudspeaker. Turning down the tape recorder's 'treble' or 'tone' control removes some of the high-pitched hissing noise.

A vibrating ruler

Place a ruler on a table, so that some of the ruler hangs out over the table's edge. Press down hard on the ruler right at the edge, and 'twang' the ruler so that it makes a sound. You can see it vibrating.

How can you make the sound higher or lower in pitch?

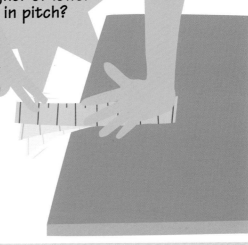

What's going on?

The longer you make the vibrating part of the ruler, the slower it vibrates, and the lower the pitch of the sound.

ON THE ALERT

Very high-pitched sounds (ultrasound) cannot be heard by human beings at all, but can be heard by some animals. This dog's ears are pricked up to hear sounds its owner may not even notice. If the animal hears anything to suggest danger, it will bark loudly as a warning.

Musical sounds

Music is sound that has a pleasing mixture of different vibrations. Musical notes have particular frequencies of vibration. Musical instruments are divided into three types, depending upon how the sound is produced. There are percussion instruments, such as drums and cymbals, that produce sound when they are hit. Wind instruments, such as trombones or clarinets, produce sound when the air inside them vibrates. Finally, string instruments, such as violins and guitars, have strings that produce sound when they are bowed or plucked.

Rubber band guitar

Make your own guitar, using rubber bands, some wood and a shoe box.

YOU WILL NEED

20
◆ AN EMPTY SHOE BOX
◆ LARGE RUBBER BANDS
◆ SCISSORS
◆ GLUE
◆ TWO PIECES OF WOOD, ABOUT
   1CM SQUARE AND AS WIDE
   AS THE SHOE BOX

1 Remove the lid from the shoe box, and cut a hole in the top.

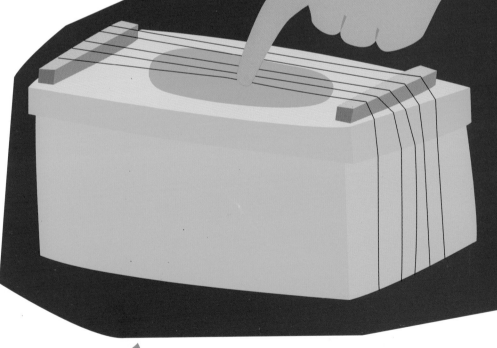

2 Using the glue, stick one piece of wood to each end of your shoe box, on either side of the hole you have cut out. Leave to dry.

3 Stretch the rubber bands across the top of the shoe box and the pieces of wood. Leave a gap of about 1cm between each rubber band. Press one finger on the rubber band at different distances while you pluck with your other hand, to play different notes.

How can you make different notes on your rubber band guitar?

What's going on?

When you pluck the rubber bands, they vibrate and make a sound. The whole box vibrates, which makes the sound louder. You can raise the pitch of the note in three ways – a rubber band will produce a higher note the more stretched it is, the shorter it is, and the thinner it is.

Pan pipes

Ask an adult to help you cut the piping into eight different lengths, between 7cm and 16cm. Make eight balls of modelling clay, each about 2cm in diameter, and press each piece over one end of each of the lengths of pipe, to make a seal. Lay the pipes next to each other, so that the open ends are level with each other, from longest to shortest. Tape the pipes together. Hold the open end of one of the pan pipes against your bottom lip and gently blow air across it.

YOU WILL NEED
20
◆ A LENGTH OF PLASTIC PIPING, ABOUT 1M LONG
◆ SCISSORS
◆ MODELLING CLAY
◆ STICKY TAPE

Which pipes produce the highest notes?

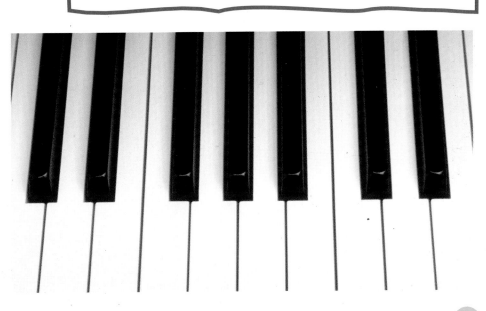

What's going on?

When you blow air across the pipes, air vibrates inside. The longer lengths of piping produce lower notes, because long columns of air vibrate more slowly. The shorter lengths produce higher notes.

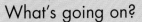

GOOD VIBRATIONS
Hitting piano keys makes wooden hammers strike the piano's steel strings. Each of the strings plays a different note. The long, heavy strings produce low notes, while the shorter, lighter strings make high notes.

White light

Most light sources, including the Sun and torches, give out 'white light'. It is given this name because it seems to have no colour. In fact, white light has more colour than any other type of light. White light is a mixture of many colours, from red to blue. In some situations, all the colours separate out to produce a continuous band of colour called the white light spectrum. For example, a rainbow forms when raindrops separate sunlight into a spectrum.

Compact spectrum

You can produce a spectrum with a compact disc. Take care when handling this not to touch or scratch the shiny surface.

YOU WILL NEED 10
- ◆ A COMPACT DISC
- ◆ A TORCH
- ◆ KITCHEN FOIL

1 Make a hole about 0.5cm in diameter in the middle of the foil. Wrap the foil over the front of the torch. Make sure that the hole is over the middle of the torch.

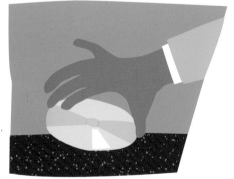

2 Place the compact disc on a table, with the writing facing downwards.

3 Turn on the torch and hold it so that light reflects off the compact disc and into your eyes. You will need to have the compact disc between you and the torch, and point the torch diagonally downwards.

What's going on?
The surface of a compact disc is covered with very small dents called pits. These cause each colour of light to reflect at a slightly different angle, producing the spectrum.

Home-made rainbow

Fill the plant sprayer with water, and set the spray to produce a fine mist. Stand with your back to the Sun. Try to face something dark, like a large bush. This experiment works best in the morning or the evening, when the Sun is not very high in the sky. Spray water in front of you. You will see a band of colours from red to violet (the spectrum) – your very own rainbow!

Can you see a rainbow?

YOU WILL NEED
5
◆ A WATER SPRAY FOR SPRAYING PLANTS
◆ A SUNNY DAY

What's going on?

You should be able to see the seven main colour regions in the spectrum – red, orange, yellow, green, blue, indigo and violet.

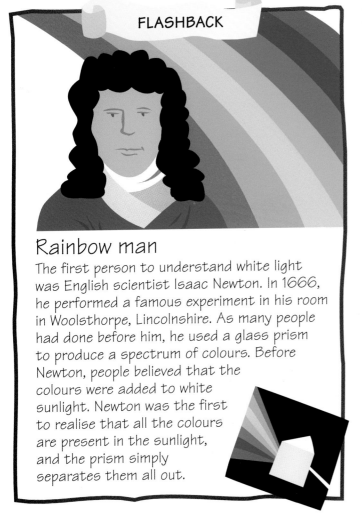

FLASHBACK

Rainbow man

The first person to understand white light was English scientist Isaac Newton. In 1666, he performed a famous experiment in his room in Woolsthorpe, Lincolnshire. As many people had done before him, he used a glass prism to produce a spectrum of colours. Before Newton, people believed that the colours were added to white sunlight. Newton was the first to realise that all the colours are present in the sunlight, and the prism simply separates them all out.

I CAN SEE A RAINBOW...

You can see the white light spectrum in a rainbow. In very bright sunshine, you can sometimes see a second rainbow above the main one. The colours are reversed in the second rainbow, with violet at the top.

Coloured light

A theatre stage can be lit up with coloured lights, by shining a white spotlight through a coloured filter. The brake lights at the back of a car look red because they shine through a red plastic filter. Filters remove certain colours from white light, but allow the rest of the spectrum through. Some light sources produce only certain colours of the spectrum.

YOU WILL NEED   10
- A GLASS BOWL FILLED WITH WATER
- A TORCH
- MILK
- A TEASPOON

Make your own sunset

Have you ever wondered why the Sun appears orange at sunset? As white light from the Sun passes through the air, the blue and green parts of the spectrum are scattered in all directions. Only the red, orange and yellow light gets through.

3 Shine the torch through the water again. What colour is the light now?

1 Shine the torch straight through the bowl of water towards you. What colour is the light?

How does the torch light change when the milk is added?

2 Add about half a teaspoon of milk to the water, and stir thoroughly.

What's going on?

Tiny particles of fat in the milk scatter blue and green light more than they scatter other colours. The same thing happens to the blue and green parts of sunlight as it passes through the air.

See red

Make the room dark. Hold a compact disc underneath and in front of the red 'stand-by' light of the electrical device. What colours do you see?

What colours are in different light sources?

What's going on?

Some light sources only give out certain colours of the spectrum. Many electrical devices have red 'stand-by' power lights, which produce only red light. This is why you will not see a spectrum.

Lose the blues

Make a spectrum using a compact disc (see page 18). Hold the yellow folder between the torch and the compact disc. This makes the torch light yellow. Is the spectrum the same?

What's going on?

When you shine white light through a yellow filter (your plastic folder) orange, red, yellow and green light pass through it. These are the colours of the spectrum that will appear on the compact disc. The torch light appears yellow because the folder absorbs the blue, indigo and violet light.

COLOURED TUBES
The coloured writing on advertising signs is created by glass tubes filled with different gases. These tubes often include the gas neon, which gives off orange and red light.

Hearing sound

When sound waves enter your ear, they make a tiny membrane of skin vibrate. These vibrations pass deep into the ear, where they are detected by nerves that send messages to the brain. Sources of sound that are very loud or are close to us make the membrane vibrate more than those that are quiet or far away. If we hear sounds that are too loud, our ears can be permanently damaged.

What's in ear?

When the eardrum moves to and fro, it vibrates three tiny bones (the smallest in your body). The last bone vibrates another membrane, in an organ called the cochlea. The cochlea is filled with fluid and is lined with tiny hairs. The vibrations pass through the fluid, and vibrate the hairs. The hairs are attached to nerves that pass on the information about the vibrations to your brain.

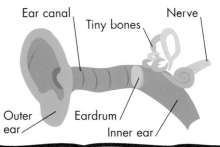

Ear canal · Tiny bones · Nerve

Outer ear · Eardrum · Inner ear

Ear drum

Sound makes a stretched rubber band vibrate, in exactly the way it causes your eardrum to vibrate.

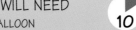

YOU WILL NEED
- A BALLOON
- SUGAR (GRANULATED)
- A GLASS OR PLASTIC TUMBLER
- SCISSORS
- AN ELASTIC BAND

10

1 Cut the balloon and open it out to form a sheet of rubber large enough to fit over the top of the tumbler.

2 Stretch the rubber sheet over the top of the tumbler, and fix it to the tumbler using the elastic band so that the sheet stays taut.

What's going on?
The sound waves hitting the rubber sheet cause it to vibrate, just as when sound hits your eardrum. You can see this because the sugar grains dance up and down.

3 Sprinkle a few sugar grains onto the rubber sheet. Now shout or make other loud noises, close to the rubber sheet. What happens to the sugar?

How can you make sugar grains dance?

Cloth ears

Play some fairly loud music, and hold the yoghurt pots over your ears. The pots absorb some of the sound, and the music does not sound so loud. Squash one sock into each yoghurt pot and hold the pots over your ears once again.

How does the music sound now?

YOU WILL NEED
◆ TWO CLEAN SOCKS
◆ A CASSETTE RECORDER
◆ TWO CLEAN, EMPTY YOGHURT POTS
5

What's going on?

The music sounds quieter because the plastic cups and the socks absorb some of the sound waves, so fewer of them reach your ears. Very loud sounds can damage your ears. People who are regularly exposed to loud noises, like factory workers, wear ear protectors that are specially designed to absorb sound.

LOUD AND QUIET

When a rocket takes off, it makes incredibly loud sounds. If you stood nearby, the sound would hurt your ears. A few kilometres away from the rocket, however, the sound is not so loud. Sound is louder the closer you are to its source, because the sound spreads out as it travels.

Seeing light

Light from light sources, or light that has reflected off other objects, enters our eyes through a lens (see pages 34–35). The lens forms a picture, called an image, at the back of the eye. The back of the eye is connected to the brain by a bundle of nerves. Our eyes hold an image of what we see for about a quarter of a second after the light has entered our eyes.

Model of the eye

To see how the eye forms an image, make a simple model, using a balloon.

YOU WILL NEED
- A BALLOON
- A SQUARE OF CARD
- SCISSORS
- A TORCH
- A MAGNIFYING GLASS
- STICKY TAPE

15

1 Fill the balloon with water from the tap until the balloon is about 10cm in diameter. Tie the balloon, so that the water cannot escape.

2 Cut a piece of card to fit over the front of the torch. Cut an arrow-shaped slit in the card, as shown, and stick the card to the front of the torch.

3 Hold the magnifying glass right in front of the balloon. Now point the torch at the balloon and turn it on.

FLASHBACK

Ideas about seeing

Most people in Ancient Egypt and Ancient Greece thought that when we looked at something, some kind of visual rays came out of our eyes, bounced off objects and then back into our eyes.

What's going on?

You should see an image of the arrow at the back of the balloon. The image is upside down, or inverted, because the magnifying glass makes the light rays cross over each other as they pass through the balloon. Images in the eye are inverted, too, but the brain interprets them so we see them the right way up.

Fooling the eye

In a dark room, turn on the lamp and hold the compact disc underneath the bulb. Look closely at the spectrum this produces. Is it a complete spectrum? What colours are missing?

YOU WILL NEED 5
◆ A COMPACT DISC
◆ A LAMP WITH AN 'ENERGY SAVING' BULB

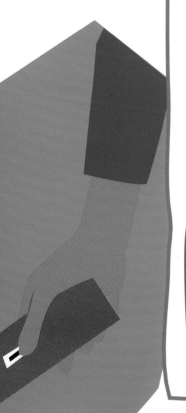

What colours do you see?

What's going on?

Fluorescent lamps, such as 'energy saving' light bulbs, appear white. But they do not produce all the colours of the spectrum, like the Sun or an incandescent lamp does. They fool the eye into seeing white, by producing red, green and blue light.

Only three colours

Turn on the television, and look closely at the screen using a magnifying glass. It has three types of dot — red, green and blue ones.

YOU WILL NEED 5
◆ A TELEVISION
◆ A MAGNIFYING GLASS

What's going on?

Believe it or not, all of the colours you see on a colour television screen are produced by mixing light of just three colours.

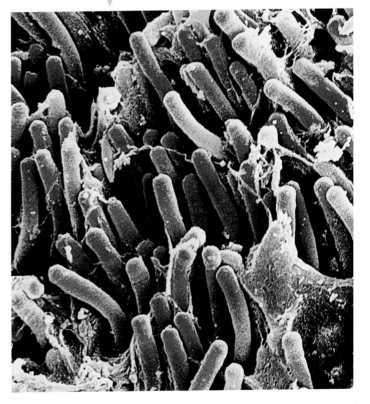

LOOK INTO MY EYES

At the back of your eye are cells that are sensitive to light. These cells send signals along nerves to your brain. Some cells are sensitive to red light, some to green, and some to blue.

Reflecting sound

When sound hits a solid object it bounces off, or reflects, just like a ball thrown against a wall. The reflected sound is called an echo. Sound travelling underground – seismic waves – reflects off layers of rock. Recording these underground echoes can tell us much about the nature of those rocks. This is called seismic surveying.

What angle?

Using two kitchen foil tubes, find out how the sound of a ticking watch reflects off a surface.

YOU WILL NEED
- A WATCH THAT TICKS
- TWO KITCHEN FOIL TUBES
- A HARD BACK BOOK

10

1 Open the book slightly, and stand it about 30cm from the edge of a table. Lay one tube on the table, with one end next to the book.

2 Hold the watch near to the other end of the tube. Some of the sound made by the watch will travel down the tube and reflect off the book.

3 Place your ear at one end of the other tube and listen for the reflected sound of the ticking watch. Where do you have to place the tube?

What's going on?

The sound of the watch travels down the tube and reflects off the book. You should be able to hear the ticking sound at only one position.

Bouncing waves

You can experience bouncing sound for yourself! Go outside, close your eyes, and say 'Hello!' quite loudly. Move a book in front of your face, about 20cm away, with the cover facing you, and say 'hello' again. Can you hear the difference? What happens if you use a woollen jumper instead of the book?

Do both of these objects reflect the sound?

What's going on?

The sound waves from your voice are reflected off the book. The jumper does not reflect the sound so well. Air pockets trapped inside the wool soak up most of the sound.

FLASHBACK

Finding their way

About 200 years ago, Italian priest and biologist Lazzaro Spallanzani came up with a very strange idea — that bats find their way around, and even hunt, using echoes. More than 100 years later, Spallanzani's idea was shown to be correct. Bats, dolphins and a few other animals do produce high-pitched sounds, and find their way around by listening to the echoes. This is called echolocation.

CONCERT HALL
Sounds made by musicians in a concert hall bounce off the walls and ceiling, causing repeated echoes, or reverberation. Too much of this can spoil the sound, so absorbent materials like curtains are used to reduce the echoes.

Reflecting light

The Moon does not produce any light of its own, and yet at Full Moon, it is almost light enough to read a book! The light that reaches Earth from the Moon is sunlight that has reflected off the Moon. Light reflects off most things, but much better off white and silvery objects than off dark ones. Some materials reflect only certain colours of light, which is why they appear coloured.

Moon shapes

It is easy to demonstrate why the shape of the illuminated Moon changes from night to night.

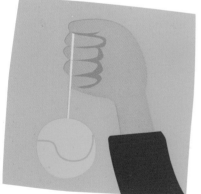

1 Tape one end of the string to the ball. Now, make the room dark.

2 Stand in the centre of the room and hold the string so that the ball is just higher than head level and in front of you, suspended in the darkness, like the Moon in space.

What does the tennis ball look like as you turn around?

YOU WILL NEED
- A TORCH
- A TENNIS BALL
- STRING ABOUT 15CM LONG
- STICKY TAPE
- A FRIEND

15

3 Ask a friend to turn on the torch and shine it at the ball. Now turn around slowly. What do you see?

What's going on?

In this experiment, the ball is a model of the Moon, the torch is the Sun and you are the Earth. The Sun always illuminates half the Moon, and the Moon travels around the Earth once every month. When the Moon is between the Earth and the Sun, we cannot see any reflected light. We call this New Moon. When the Earth is between the Sun and the Moon, we can see the whole face of the Moon. This is Full Moon.

Black and white

Place the two sheets of paper next to each other on a table next to a wall. Make the room dark, and shine the torch on to the white paper. You should see a patch of light on the wall. Now, shine the torch at the black paper.

What's going on?

The white paper reflects much more light on to the wall than the black paper does. Supermarket checkout scanners make use of this fact – a laser reflects off the black and white lines of the barcodes, and a sensor detects the reflected light.

Reflecting colours

Make the room dark, and hold the jumper next to the wall. Shine the torch at the jumper, so that light reflects off the jumper. You should see a patch of coloured light.

What's going on?

White light from the torch is a mixture of many colours. The red jumper only reflects the red light from this mixture.

FLASHBACK

Moon mirror

In 1961, astronomers in America bounced a laser beam off a mirror that astronauts had left on the Moon. By timing how long the light took to return, they worked out the distance to the moon to an accuracy of just a few metres.

ROAD REFLECTOR SIGN
Some road signs are made from materials that reflect light from the headlights of approaching traffic. Different parts of the sign reflect different colours, giving drivers a clear bright image of hazards ahead.

Mirrors

Have you ever caught your reflection in a shop window? Any shiny surface can act as a mirror, but the mirrors in a bathroom or in your bedroom at home reflect all of the light that falls on them. The picture, or image, in a mirror is reversed – right becomes left and left becomes right. Curved mirrors can make things become reversed, too. They can also make things look bigger, smaller or even upside down.

Seeing it both ways

A piece of clear plastic can act as a mirror – on both sides.

Which of the faces you see is a reflection, and which is not?

YOU WILL NEED
- A FLAT SHEET OF CLEAR PLASTIC FROM A PICTURE FRAME
- A TORCH
- A FRIEND

10

1 In a dark room, sit or stand facing your friend, about one metre away from him or her. Hold the plastic vertically, halfway between you.

2 Turn on the torch and shine it at your face. You should see a reflection of yourself in the plastic. What does your friend see?

3 Ask your friend to shine the torch on his or her face. Now you should see your friend's face, because the light has bounced off it and passed through the plastic. But what does your friend see?

What's going on?

Most of the light that hits a clear plastic or glass surface passes through – this is why you can see your friend in step 3. Some light reflects off the plastic surface, and when there is no light passing through from the other side, you can see the reflected light. This is why you see yourself in step 2.

Magic window picture

Face a window and hold the paper up in front of your face. Now hold the mirror so that it faces away from you and light from the window reflects on to the paper. Make the distance between the mirror and the paper about 15cm. You should be able to see an image of the window on the paper. Alter the distance between the mirror and the paper if you do not see the image straight away.

YOU WILL NEED
- A MAGNIFYING MAKE-UP OR SHAVING MIRROR
- A PIECE OF WHITE PAPER

10

Can you produce an image on paper with your mirror?

What's going on?
Because the mirror curves inwards, light is brought together, or focussed. This is how it is possible to produce a bright image on the paper.

Reflect on this

Hold the mirror close to your face. The image will be large and the right way up. Scary! Now get your friend to hold the mirror at arm's length, between one and two metres from your face. This time, the image will be smaller and upside down, or inverted.

YOU WILL NEED
- A MAGNIFYING MAKE-UP OR SHAVING MIRROR
- A FRIEND

5

What's going on?
Mirrors that are used to help people shave or do their make-up are curved inwards (they are called concave mirrors). A concave mirror produces an enlarged view of an object but only if the object is held close to the mirror.

LIQUID MIRRORS
Believe it or not, this mirror is made of liquid metal (mercury). It is going to be used in a telescope. Most telescopes use curved mirrors made of glass or solid metal. This liquid one actually makes a better reflecting surface because mercury produces a perfect dish shape, reflecting all the light that hits it.

Bending light

At the swimming pool, you may have noticed that people swimming underwater look different from how they look out of the water. Light that has reflected off their bodies bends as it leaves the water. This bending of light is called refraction, and happens whenever light passes from one transparent substance to another.

Watch it bend

In this experiment, you can watch a beam of light bending as it enters a bowl of water.

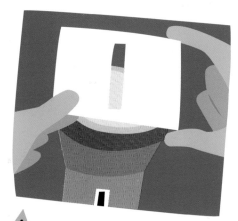

1 Cut a piece of card that will cover the front of the torch. Make a slit in the middle of the card, about 0.5cm wide. Tape the piece of card over the torch.

2 Add a few drops of milk to the water and mix it in well.

YOU WILL NEED
- A TORCH
- CARD, STICKY TAPE AND SCISSORS
- A GLASS BOWL FILLED WITH WATER
- MILK

15

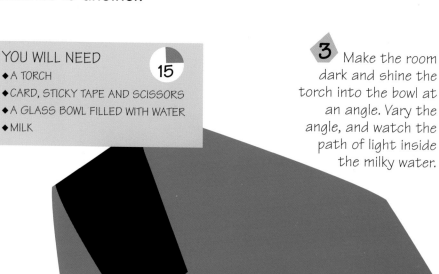

Why does the beam of light bend as it enters the bowl?

What's going on?
The milk in the water allows you to see the path of the light. You will see the light bend as it enters the bowl. This is because as the beam of light moves from air into the glass and milky water, it changes direction slightly.

3 Make the room dark and shine the torch into the bowl at an angle. Vary the angle, and watch the path of light inside the milky water.

Now you don't see it...

Using the modelling clay, attach the coin to the bottom of the saucepan at the opposite side from you. Move your head to the height where the coin just disappears from view. Slowly fill the pan with water. The coin slowly comes into view, without you having to move your head!

YOU WILL NEED
- A SAUCEPAN
- MODELLING CLAY
- WATER
- A COIN

5

Why does it look as if the coin moves under the water?

What's going on?
Refraction occurs when light passes from water to air. This can change the way things look under water.

More or less

Find somewhere lit up by bright sunlight. If it is not sunny, use the torch. Fill the dish with water, and place it where light shines into the water. Stand the mirror against one end of the dish, sloping as shown. Now hold the paper vertically in front of the dish, so that light reflecting off the mirror hits it. You may even see a patch of light on the wall.

YOU WILL NEED
- A SUNNY DAY OR A TORCH
- A FLAT MIRROR
- A FLAT DISH
- WATER
- WHITE PAPER

10

What's going on?
Sunlight (or light from the torch) is a mixture of many colours. Each colour of light refracts at a slightly different angle, so the colours spread out, forming a bright spectrum of colours which you see reflected on the paper.

AFTER IMAGE
Believe it or not, this photograph was taken after the Sun had set! It was possible because light refracts as it passes from the vacuum of space into the atmosphere. Light from the Sun hits the top of the atmosphere, and refracts downwards towards people on the ground.

Lenses

You may know that cameras, binoculars, slide projectors and microscopes use lenses. Have you ever wondered how a lens works? Lenses are specially-shaped pieces of transparent material (usually glass) that can make things look bigger, smaller, nearer or farther away, than they really are or even upside down. And all because light refracts as it passes through the lens.

Slide projector

A lens can project an image on to a wall. You can even use a lens to make a simple slide projector, making a drawing appear much bigger than it really is.

1 Make the room dark. Turn on the lamp and hold the paper over it. Do not hold it too close, as the lamp could be hot.

What's going on?
Light from the lamp passes through the paper and then it refracts as it passes through the magnifying glass. An image of the paper will only form on the wall or ceiling if the magnifying glass is at just the right distance from the paper.

FLASHBACK

Eyeglass
Some people wear contact lenses to correct their vision. Contact lenses were invented in 1887 by a German inventor, Adolf Fick. They were made of glass and were very uncomfortable. Modern plastic lenses were introduced in 1948, and today, even disposable contact lenses are available.

YOU WILL NEED
- A MAGNIFYING GLASS
- A DESK LAMP
- A PIECE OF PAPER WITH A LARGE DRAWING ON IT

10

Can you see the drawing on the wall or the ceiling?

2 Now, hold the magnifying glass about 10cm above or in front of the paper. You should see an image of the drawing on the ceiling or the wall.

What magnification?

Draw a line 1cm long on the paper. Look at the line through the magnifying glass and try to draw how big the line looks. Measure the line you have drawn.

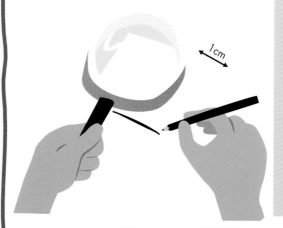

1cm

What's going on?
A magnifying glass is a type of lens used to look at very small things. The length of the line (in cm) is the magnification of the magnifying glass. If the line was 2.5cm long, your magnifying glass has a magnification of 2.5x.

Water lens
Place the water on a picture in the magazine. Look at the picture through the drop. What do you see?

What's going on?
A drop of water is a simple lens. It can make things look bigger (magnify them) or make them look as though they are far away. Light from an object passes through the water and refracts, making an image of the object. The type of image depends upon whether the object is far from or close to the lens.

A FARAWAY LIGHT
The glass around the light in a lighthouse is made up of a series of glass rings which form a lens. This concentrates the light so that it projects brightly and over long distances.

Recording sound and light

It is easy to take for granted photographs, television, film, and sound recordings of people talking or our favourite music. When sound hits a microphone, the microphone produces an electric current that flows back and forth in the same way as the vibrations of the sound. Light is normally recorded on a light-sensitive film in a camera. Camcorders and digital cameras contain an electronic device called a charge coupled device, or CCD. Like a microphone, it produces an electric current.

YOU WILL NEED
◆ A CASSETTE PLAYER WITH A MICROPHONE SOCKET
◆ AN EMPTY 35MM FILM CANISTER
◆ A 3.5MM AUDIO JACK PLUG (MONO), ALREADY CONNECTED TO A CABLE
◆ STICKY TAPE
◆ A SMALL BAR MAGNET
◆ A BLANK CASSETTE
◆ ABOUT 1.5M OF INSULATED WIRE, WITH ABOUT 1CM OF THE INSULATION STRIPPED OFF EACH END

20

Make a microphone

If you have a cassette player that has a microphone socket, you can use a home-made microphone to record the sound of your own voice! Ask an adult to help you collect the things you need, and to help you put the experiment together.

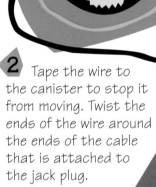

1 Wrap the wire around the canister at least 30 times, leaving about 10cm free at each end.

2 Tape the wire to the canister to stop it from moving. Twist the ends of the wire around the ends of the cable that is attached to the jack plug.

3 Plug the jack plug into the microphone socket of the cassette player and insert the cassette.

4 Start the machine recording, hold the magnet just inside the open end of the canister, and shout as loudly as you can into the canister.

FLASHBACK

The TALKIES

When you go to the cinema, you can hear the voices of the actors in the film, and music and sound effects, too. The first films had no sound — they were 'silent movies'. The first 'talking picture', or film with sound on general release was 'The Jazz Singer', released in 1928. Audiences at the time were stunned to hear the voice of the star of the film, singer Al Jolson, whose first words in the film were 'You ain't heard nothing yet'.

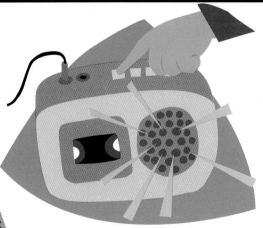

5 Stop and rewind the tape. When you play back at loud volume, you should be able to hear your voice, very faintly, recorded on the tape.

What's going on?
The sound of your voice vibrates the film canister and the coiled wire. Since there is a magnet inside the coil, this causes a small electric current to flow backwards and forwards in the wire. The current is a copy of the vibrations produced by your voice.

Make your own photograph

Cut away some shapes in the piece of black paper. In a darkened room, take a piece of photographic paper, and lay the black paper and your chosen objects on it. Point the lamp at the paper, turn it on, and leave it for a few minutes. Switch the lamp off, and take the objects off the paper. You have your own home-made photograph!

YOU WILL NEED
- A PACKET OF PHOTOGRAPHIC PAPER
- A PIECE OF BLACK PAPER
- A LAMP
- A PENCIL
- SCISSORS
- A SELECTION OF SMALL, FLAT OBJECTS

What happens to the picture after a few minutes?

What's going on?
The photographic paper contains chemicals which are sensitive to light. The parts the light reaches change, but the parts covered by the objects and black paper do not.

DIGITAL CAMERA
A recent invention of the electronics industry is the digital camera. Inside a digital camera is a CCD (charge coupled device). Light passes through a lens in the camera, forming an image on the CCD. The image is converted into a pattern of electric currents that can be read by a computer, and displayed on a computer screen.

Glossary

Barcode   Series of numbers with vertical black and white lines often found on the packaging or labels of products. When a barcode is scanned at the checkout, a laser reflects off the lines of the barcode and a sensor detects the pattern of the reflected light. This pattern gives information about that particular product and its price.

CCD   Short for charge coupled device. A device found in a digital camera that converts an image from the camera lens into a pattern of electrical currents that can be read by a computer and displayed on a computer screen.

Cell   The smallest basic unit in the structure of living things. All cells have a watery jelly-like substance inside them called cytoplasm, and are surrounded by a membrane. Different parts of our bodies are made up of different types of cell. All cells use energy so they can function and reproduce.

Cochlea   A spiral-shaped part of the inner ear, which contains fluid and many thousands of hairs. The fluid and hairs vibrate when sound travels through them, then nerves pick up this information and pass it on to the brain. The brain then interprets the signals it receives as sound.

Concave mirror   A mirror whose reflective surface curves inwards.

Ear defenders   Protective coverings for the ears that people wear in noisy places like factories to prevent damage to their hearing. Ear defenders are made of material containing lots of air holes, which help to absorb loud noises.

Eardrum   A tiny membrane of skin inside the ear that vibrates when sound waves enter the ear. The vibrations are passed deeper into the ear and are detected by nerves which send messages to the brain, where they are interpreted as sound.

Echolocation   A way of finding the position of something by sending out sounds which are reflected back from it. Bats, dolphins and some other birds make use of this. They make high-pitched sounds and use the echoes to find their way around.

Filament   A thin metal wire in a light bulb. The filament heats up to high temperatures when electricity passes through. This causes it to produce light through incandescence.

Filter   A clear screen, through which light can pass, that removes certain colours from white light, allowing the rest of the spectrum through.

Fluorescent   Light given out by some materials when they absorb various kinds of energy. The inside of a fluorescent lamp is coated with a material that absorbs ultraviolet light and changes it into visible light.

Focus   A way of bringing something together and concentrating it in one place, as when light is focussed in a concave mirror.

Frequency   How often something happens. For example, a source of sound that vibrates many times a second has a high frequency.

Image   A picture or likeness of a person or thing produced from a mirror, through a lens or by electrical means on a screen.

Incandescence   Light given out from objects, such as the Sun, because they are hot. An incandescent lamp produces light because its electrical filament becomes hot.

Lens   Specially-shaped pieces of transparent material that can make things look bigger, smaller, nearer or farther away. They do this by bending the light as it passes into them and out again.

Luminescence   Light given out from objects, such as fireflies and television screens, produced by means other than heat.

Membrane   A thin, flexible piece of skin which joins or covers parts of a living thing, or separates one part of a living thing from another.

Neon   A colourless gas that glows orange and red when electricity is passed through it. It is often used in glass tube lighting for advertising signs.

Nerve   A pathway that carries messages between the brain and other parts of the body.

Pitch   The way something sounds high or low, like the different notes in a musical scale.

Prism   A transparent block of glass or plastic with several sides which can separate light passing through it into the colours of the spectrum.

Reflection   The bouncing back of light or sound from a surface, for example light from a mirror, or sound from the walls of the inside of a tunnel.

Refraction   The way light bends as it passes from one different substance to another, for example from air to water or from air to glass.

Seismic waves   Sound waves travelling underground which reflect off layers of rock. These can be recorded to help show what type of rock is found in a particular area and to study the effects of earthquakes.

Shock wave   A disturbance in the air that travels out in all directions. It is a sound wave that is heard as a loud sound when it reaches your ears. The sound of thunder is produced by a shock wave.

Source   The place from which sound or light comes, for example the Sun is a source of light, and a cassette player is a source of sound. The energy of both sound and light travels by means of waves.

Spectrum   A band of colours that together make up white light but that can sometimes be separated out, for example by raindrops or a prism, into the seven colour regions seen in rainbows – red, orange, yellow, green, blue, indigo and violet.

Translucent   A material is translucent if it lets some light through, but not clearly enough that you can see through it.

Transparent   A material is transparent if it lets nearly all the light through, so you can see through it clearly.

Triboluminescence   The giving out of light from something when it is rubbed, scratched or broken.

Ultrasound   Sounds with very rapid vibrations whose pitch is too high to be heard by humans. Some animals can hear ultrasound.

Vibration   Something moving very quickly backwards and forwards. Sound is produced because of vibrations in the air. Sometimes vibrations can be felt as well as heard.

Vocal cords   A pair of membranes found in the larynx, or voice box. When we breathe air into them from the lungs, they vibrate and produce the sound of our voice. This sound varies in pitch, depending on whether the cords vibrate quickly (high sounds) or slowly (low sounds).

Wave   A disturbance of the air. Waves travel from a source of sound in all directions. When they reach your ears, you hear a sound. It is useful to picture sound waves travelling through the air like ripples on a pond.

Index